...ngs to...

The
Wild Fruit Fairies

Illustrated by

Margaret W. Tarrant

Original poetry by

Marion St. John Webb

Series Editor
Fiona Waters

·MARGARET TARRANT'S·

FAIRIES & FLOWERS

First published in this format in 2002 by
The Medici Society Ltd
Grafton House, Hyde Estate Road, London NW9 6JZ

Copyright © The Medici Society Ltd 2002 / 1925

First published in 1925 by The Medici Society Ltd
3 5 7 9 10 8 6 4 2

The rights of Margaret Tarrant and Marion St John Webb to be identified
as the Illustrator and Author of this work have been asserted by them in
accordance with the Copyright, Design and Patents Act 1988.

A catalogue record for this book is available from the British Library.

ISBN 0 85503 257 X

Margaret Tarrant's original artworks have been rescanned for this re-designed edition.

Designed by Tony Potter Publishing Ltd

Printed in Singapore

The Wild Fruit Fairies

Contents

A Bit of Magic

Cross your middle fingers,
　　Stand upon your toes.
That's a bit of magic,
Not everybody knows.

If you see a fairy,
Do not make a noise;
Fairies are suspicious
Of little girls and boys.

Look! The magic's working!
Hiding in the grass,
Can't you see the fairy?
Did you see her pass?

All among the bushes
Blackberries are ripe.
Look! There's another fairy,
Playing a silver pipe!

Here's a little goblin
Lying fast asleep;
Blackberries he's gathered,
Left them in a heap.

See the tiny fairies
Stealing from his pile?
Won't there be some trouble
In a little while!

There's a little fairy
Whispering on the breeze.
Fairies in the hedges,
Fairies in the trees.

They are all around us,
But we couldn't see,
Until we tried the magic
Made by you and me.

Blue Wings

A fairy grew tired
    With the colour of her wings,
They were pink and silver,
Sweet and dainty things.
"I want a different colour.
I'd like a purply-blue."
And so she looked around
To see what she could do.

She picked some whortleberries;
And then she thought a while.
She squeezed their juice most gently
And gave a little smile.
"Now I'll dye my wings and they will be
Just the colour that I wish."
And she stirred the juice round and round
Inside a little dish.

She dipped her wings and dyed them,
In the whortleberry stain,
Dried them in the moonlight,
Then flew back home again.
And all her seven sisters
Clapped their hands in great delight,
And went and dyed their wings as well,
That very same night.

And so the fashion started,
And then it grew and grew,
Till everyone in fairyland
Had wings of purply-blue!

Strawberry Jam

A basketful of strawberries,
 Red and sweet and small,
Tip them in the fairy pot,
Stalks and leaves and all.
Pour the wild bee's honey in,
Stir it round and round.
Cook it on a fire of sticks
Built upon the ground.

Bubble! Bubble!
Now the jam is cooking.
Bubble! Bubble!
Is anybody looking?
Could a little fairy
Who hasn't had his tea,
Take a tiny taste of jam?
Would anybody see?

A basketful of strawberries,
Cook and stir and skim.
Get the little acorn cups,
Fill them to the brim.
Fairy jam-pots acorns make,
With a leaf for lid.
Stand them in a row to cool.
This the fairies did.

Trouble! Trouble!
Fairy cooks are sleeping.
Trouble! Trouble!
Someone here comes creeping.
Here's a little fairy now,
Who hasn't had his tea.
Takes a little pot of jam,
Did anybody see?

The Enchanted Earrings

A pair of magic earrings
   Were growing on a tree.
Then someone picked those earrings
For all the world to see.
A pair of cherry earrings,
As magic as could be.

The Bucket Fairy picked them,
(She lived inside a well)
She wanted magic earrings,
As all the world could tell,
She wore those magic earrings
As she sat inside her well.

The Cherry Fairies told her
As she sat inside her well,
"You'll *hear* the sun shining,
It is the truth we tell.
Who ever wears those earrings
Lets loose a magic spell."

The Bucket Fairy wore them
An earring on each ear.
She said, "I've magic earrings!"
So all the world could hear.
She sat inside her bucket
And listened for a year.

She sat inside her bucket
Although it crushed her dress.
The Cherry Fairies teased her,
But she never would confess
If she *could* hear the sunshine.
She left them all to guess.

Pebble in the Lane

The Raspberry Fairies have a game
 They often like to play.
They count the seeds in a raspberry,
In the "tinker tailor" way.
Singing, "moonbeam, starlight,
Sunshine, rain,
Dewdrop, snowflake,
Pebble in the lane."

There is a little fairy, very quiet and shy,
Who doesn't like the game.
She counts the seeds in the raspberries
And they always come the same.
Never "moonbeam," "starlight,"
"Sunshine," "rain."
She always gets
"Pebble in the lane!"

Bunching, Crunching and
Mumberly-Hatch

Bunching, Crunching and
Mumberly-Hatch
Old Crab-Apple Dwarfs would meet
Up in the tree-tops, or under the thatch,
Down in the garden, out in the street;
Whatever the time, wherever the place
It never concerned them, they were a disgrace.
Bunching, Crunching and Mumberly-Hatch
Went shouting away in a breathless race.

Bunching, Crunching and Mumberly-Hatch,
Those Crab-Apple Dwarfs would boast
Each to the other, "I have no match!"
Gathering moonbeams or buttering toast,
Whichever it was, whatever the test,
Each boaster declared he outshone the rest.
Bunching, Crunching and Mumberly-Hatch
Each said that he voted himself the best.

Bunching, Crunching and Mumberly-Hatch,
Three Crab-Apple Dwarfs, every day
Talking and arguing, ready to snatch
Each from the other, the words he would say
And now it's the custom throughout the
land
To call any boaster in Fairyland,
"Bunching", "Crunching", or
    "Mumberly-Hatch".
And all boasters grow silent as they
    understand.

Margaret Winifred Tarrant (1888 - 1959)

'Every time a child says, " I don't believe in
fairies," ' warned Peter Pan, 'there is a little fairy
somewhere that falls down dead.' By her
paintings Margaret Tarrant did as much to
encourage children's belief in fairies as J M
Barrie did by his writings. Born in London in
1888, the only child of artist Percy
Tarrant and his wife Sarah,
Margaret excelled at art from
an early age, and she was only
19 when she received her
first, very prestigious,
commission, from J M Dent
& Sons: to illustrate Charles
Kingsley's much-loved
children's classic, *The Water Babies*,
which was first published in 1863.

Her delicate, charming pictures matched the
spirit of the story perfectly and earned her a
string of new commissions: *Nursery Rhymes* (1914
and 1923), *Alice in Wonderland* (1916) and

Hans Andersen's Fairy Tales (1917) for Ward Lock & Co., plus postcards for Oxford University Press.

Margaret Tarrant illustrated some 20 books for George G. Harrap & Co. between 1915 and 1929, but an even more important publishing relationship began in 1920, when she completed her first pieces for The Medici Society. This was to prove a long and fruitful connection, resulting in most of her best-known work. In the 1920s, for example, she illustrated this highly successful series of fairy books for the company, written by the poet and author Marion St John Webb. Her picture of Peter's Friends, inspired by J M Barrie's *Peter Pan* stories and the statue in Kensington Gardens, proved so popular when it appeared in 1921 that it had to be reproduced many times.

Peter's Friends

The dusk of the nineteenth and dawn of the twentieth centuries were magical times for fairy lovers. Fascination with fairy lore was widespread, reaching unprecedented heights in 1922 when Sir Arthur Conan Doyle published *The Coming of the Fairies*, containing 'photographs' of fairies taken by two young girls in a Yorkshire village, which were later proved to be hoaxes. The story was actually a fascinating deception, which was believed by many reputable people. The mystery was not solved until towards the end of the twentieth century, when the girls involved, now elderly ladies, explained what had really happened.

In 1922, Margaret Tarrant's *Do You Believe in Fairies?* showed two children encircled by a ring of fairies, which caught the public excitement already created by Sir Arthur Conan Doyle's book.

Do You Believe in Fairies?

This interest was mirrored in an outpouring of art and literature. Children's books cultivated belief in fairies: they were used in religious teaching, magazines were devoted to them, and captivating new works appeared, most notably J M Barrie's *Peter Pan* and *Peter Pan in Kensington Gardens*. Rudyard Kipling wrote *Rewards and Fairies* and even Beatrix Potter embraced the subject in *The Fairy Caravan*.

Artists revelled in the opportunity to portray imaginary worlds. Arthur Rackham, the most fashionable illustrator of his day, depicted a sinister fantasy landscape, peopled by spiky goblins, fairies and mice amid gnarled trees with gnomelike faces. In contrast, Honor Appleton, Maud Tindal Atkinson and Mabel Lucie Atwell offered gentler, comforting images recalling Kate Greenaway's illustrations of apple-cheeked children.

Margaret Tarrant was one of those most associated with the depiction of fairies in the 1920s and 1930s, together with her friend and sketching partner, Cicely Mary Barker (1895 - 1973). Both began to use Art Nouveau and Arts and Crafts

elements in their work, and in Tarrant's paintings a breathtaking attention to detail - diaphanous wings with the intricate tracery of a dragonfly's wings - is a testament to the reality of fairies, imaginary or otherwise.

During her life Margaret Tarrant tackled a wide range of subjects and won special acclaim for those, such as *All Things Wise and Wonderful*, with a religious theme. But her forte was fairies, for in her evocation of these ethereal figures she could express her love for children, wild flowers and dance, of all that was beautiful and pure.

She would sketch meticulously from life to capture the likeness of a child or plant, then compose her pictures by arranging the subjects in imaginary settings, infusing them with a distinctive otherworldly quality.

Margaret Tarrant's fairies have a unique fluidity and balletic grace that expressed her delight in the free-flowing dance invented by Isadora Duncan. She was very much a free spirit herself, flying along the country lanes around her home in Surrey on an ancient bicycle, leaping off impulsively to sketch a flower or help a toddler to paint. She never married, but she attracted many friends by her generosity, energy and zest for life. Perhaps it was this childlike enthusiasm and innocence, combined with a special kind of imagination, that gave her a natural affinity with fairies.

The Lily Pool

Much missed when she died in 1959, Margaret Tarrant left a lasting legacy in charming pictures that seem as fresh today as the day they were painted, and still enchant new generations with their glimpses into a secret fairy world.

The new edition

There are 12 beautiful fairy books by Margaret Tarrant, originally published between 1923 - 1928. The re-designed edition is now available to collect as a set, with modern scanning methods used to bring out the exquisite detail of the original paintings and drawings.

WATER FAIRIES

TWILIGHT FAIRIES

WEATHER FAIRIES

ORCHARD FAIRIES

WILD FRUIT FAIRIES

INSECT FAIRIES

HOUSE FAIRIES

FOREST FAIRIES

SEED FAIRIES

SEASHORE FAIRIES

FLOWER FAIRIES

HEATH FAIRIES

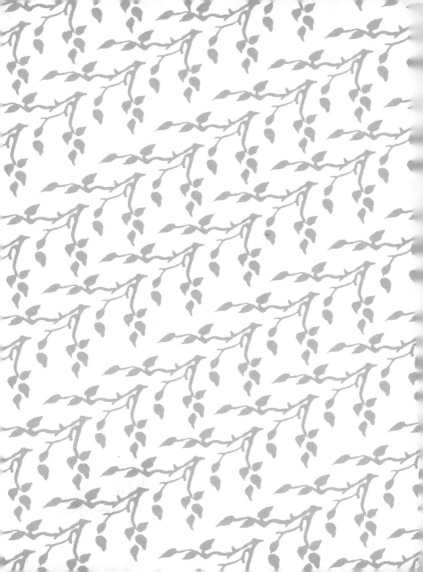